Transforming Culture

Etsko Schuitema

INTENT PUBLISHING

Published and distributed by: Schuitema Group (Pty) Ltd, trading as Intent Publishing

Postal address: PO Box 877, Walkerville, 1876

Physical Address: 64 Cross Road, Walkers Fruit Farms, De Deur, 1884

Tel: +27 11 867 0587

E-mail: info@schuitemagroup.com *Website:* www.schuitemagroup.com

Original Cover design by: Etsko Schuitema *Illustrations by:* Kayla Q (Via Fiverr)

Formatting and Cover Layout by: Colin Vermaak (Write, Learn and Earn)

Print ISBN: 978-0-6397-6364-4

Ebook ISBN: 978-0-6397-6365-1

About our logo:

The square in the middle represents The One, from The One come the two surrounding lines, the 'Outward' and the 'Inward'. The next four are the 'Sensory' and 'Meaning' aspects of the 'Inward' and 'Outward', and the last eight the 'Celestial' and 'Terrestrial' manifestations of the previous aspects.

Contents

Acknowledgments

I want to acknowledge Almas Mahmoud, and Kim Vermaak (Write, Learn and Earn) for their generous assistance in preparing this book for print and on-line.

Etsko Schuitema

Chapter 1

INTRODUCTION

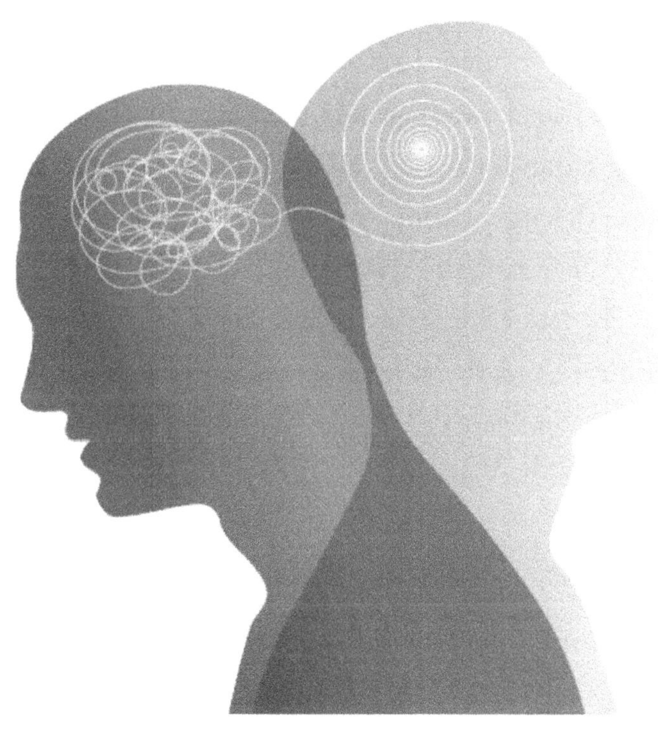

The purpose of this booklet is to summarise the core thinking of the *Care & Growth* Thematic to understand the problem of transforming culture. Although transforming culture includes a whole range of considerations, it is important to bear in mind that the core of the matter is, in fact, the individual. To be precise about the matter, we should say the following: Transforming organisational culture is concerned with transforming the intent of the individual. This is because anything you do from a culture transformation point of view that does not transform the individual and his/her habitual ways of interacting will be cosmetic in character. It may look and sound fancy, but will not have a meaningful impact. So, when dealing with the issue of culture transformation, it is essential to establish the line of sight between the organisation as a whole and the individual human being within the organisation. We have to establish the link between the "macro-change" we want to see and the "micro-changes" that in fact constitute it. And, these "micro-changes" in fact sit at the level of the intent of the individual.

One should remember that the culture of the organisation is not defined by the systems and structures of the organisation. The culture of the organisation is in fact defined by the manner in which people conduct themselves within the organisation. This means to say that systems and structures do not produce culture. Systems and structures and the product of culture. For example, an organisation populated by empowering leaders will have empowering systems and structures. It is the intent of the leaders, which produces the systems and structures, and not the other way around. This suggests that one needs to look at the issue of culture as a verb and not a noun. Culture is something we do. It lives and breathes in our conduct and the intentions behind our conduct. It is also something that moves and continuously evolves.

When we recognise this, we come to better understand how challenging it is to meaningfully transform a culture, particularly in large organisations. To meaningfully transform a culture, you have to effectively transform a large number of individuals at scale. This is a substantial challenge. But the rewards for pulling it off are potentially immense. Peter Drucker's famous quote that 'Culture eats strategy for breakfast' articulates a truism that underlines the power of culture transformation. How often does one see beautifully thought out and articulated strategies suffer shipwreck on a spirit of disengagement and lack of commitment? This means that the best of plans and strategies can be ruined on the rocks of a toxic culture. And, not only can a toxic culture shipwreck a good plan; conversely, a *healthy culture* can turn a bad plan into a monumental success.

Unfortunately, one of the biggest obstacles to transforming culture is all the complexities people build into the notion of what culture is. Many people see culture as something that has many moving parts. A single definition from a consultancy specializing in culture would suffice to demonstrate the case: "The Business Achievers indicate that

'Organizational Culture' is the collection of values, expectations, and practices that guide and inform actions of all team members." And clearly, this is not what culture is. For the most part, these things are just words we put on a wall. The actual culture just is the manner in which people actually conduct themselves and the intentions that sit behind that conduct.

It would be helpful, therefore, to arrive at a more pointed understanding of culture, one that would then enable us to readily distinguish between toxic and healthy organisational cultures. We may start however by considering a couple of the features of a *healthy culture* in order to demonstrate a point.

Here are two features of what constitutes a *healthy culture:*

- An organisation with a healthy culture will have a *spirit of collaboration* between employees that encourages innovation.

- An organisation with a healthy culture will be *customer-focused*, such that employees readily go the extra mile in delighting the customer.

What we should notice about both of these descriptions of a healthy culture is that they are both manifestations of a single variable, namely the intent of the individual in the . In the first instance, collaboration just is the intent to set my colleague up for success. This is what it means to collaborate. In the second instance, customer-focus just is the intent to be of service to the customer. Both of these then are manifestations of what we could call the Intent to Give in the individual concerned.

We see then that the degree to which the average person in the organisation interacts with the Intent to Give is the degree to which the organisation will be customer focused, innovative, and manifest a spirit of collaboration amongst its employees. And this will be the case for variables that could conceivably be considered from a culture point of view because all culture is concerned with the conduct or actions of individuals and all actions have an intention that sits behind them.

From this then we can distill the following principle:

> The culture of an organisation is toxic based on the degree to which the average member is there to take and it is healthy based on the degree to which that person is there to give.

But, what is the connection between culture understood in this way and the success of the organisation? Well, if one, for example, argues that successful organisations are profitable, then one needs to examine how enterprises produce profits or surpluses. And, when we examine where profits or surpluses actually come from, we see that the Intent to Give not only defines what it means to have a healthy culture, but it also accounts for the possibility of a profit or surplus.

We have a thought experiment that demonstrates the case which we call the 3 baker's analogy:

Let us assume that we have three bakers who collaborate to bake a cake. The cake takes them an entire month to bake and at the end of the month, each baker takes a slice home to feed his family. If there was a slice left over, we would call that slice a surplus or a profit. Now, it is important to understand that the surplus slice only exists because the total cake that was baked was bigger than what each baker took home. This means then that collectively they gave more than what they took. The surplus is, in fact, the cumulative effect of each baker giving more than they took. If each baker took as much as they gave, there would be no surplus. If each baker took more than they gave, there would be a deficit. So the willingness of the individual to make a discretionary effort (or give more than they take) in pursuit of the organisation's objectives is the primary variable that accounts for the success of organisations and is what defines the culture of the organisation.

In his book *'The Leader's Ladder'*, my colleague Bengt Savén describes the person who is willing to go the extra mile as a person who ***delivers, improves,*** and ***learns***. We understand *'delivers'* to mean a person who commits to providing what the customer or client requires, on time and in full or better than that. By *'improves'*, we consider a person who is continuously searching for better and more effective ways of delighting the customer or client. And by *'learns'*, we consider a person who stays curious about their craft and is continuously refining their skill and knowledge.

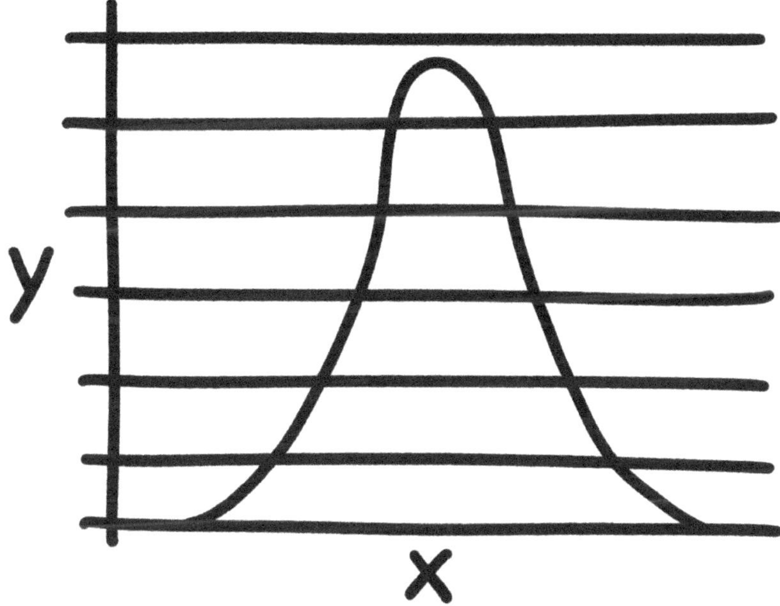

All work on culture should be concerned with enabling people like this, people who are committed to make a discretionary contribution to the organisation, who strive to deliver, improve, and learn. However, we need to accommodate the truth that not all people are the same, and that the culture of any organisation is an average. Like any bell curve, this average will be made up of a mass of people in the middle and then some outliers on either end, where there are some people who are less altruistic than most and some who are more so. We can therefore rephrase the intent of culture work to be to shift the average in the direction of those who are more inclined to give from those who are less inclined to do so.

In this work, one needs to consider the following *four* concerns:

Personal Excellence

One needs to examine whether it is possible for people to be here to give, particularly in a world where we have assumed that self-interest rules, that **"What's In It For Me"** is the cardinal truth of the human condition. We need to account for those few sunny souls who, even in the most toxic environments, stay true to a personal commitment to do their best, to deliver, improve and learn. We need to examine how their intent operates and how they approach their day-to-day work life in such a way as to have a fulfilling work experience.

Team Excellence

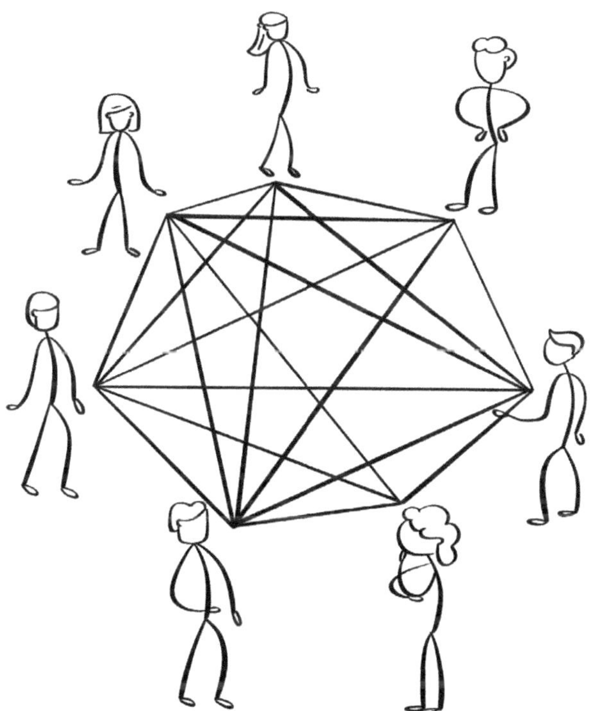

We next need to understand how this person would deal with colleagues, the intent and behaviour that they would bring to the team that would enhance a collaborative rather than a competitive engagement with teammates. This is arguably still an element that sits in the hands of the individual. We have all experienced toxic work cultures that were made more tolerable by individuals, not necessarily higher in the hierarchy, who deliberately sought to make the lives of their colleagues better. Similarly, we have all been in positive work environments that were soured by the meanness, pettiness, and competitiveness of an individual.

Leadership Excellence

Having understood the individual who is here to contribute, we now need to turn to the enablers of such a person, and the primary enabler is the leader. I think it is true that people do not go the extra mile for organisations, people go the extra mile for people. If we really want to understand the conditions under which the average person in the organisation will be more likely to come to work to contribute, we need to examine the role of the boss.

In this examination, we need to account for **two** things:

- The intent of the boss. What is the primary concern of a leader who cultivates people who are here to contribute?

- The key things that boss would do in order to cultivate people who are here to contribute.

Organisational Excellence:

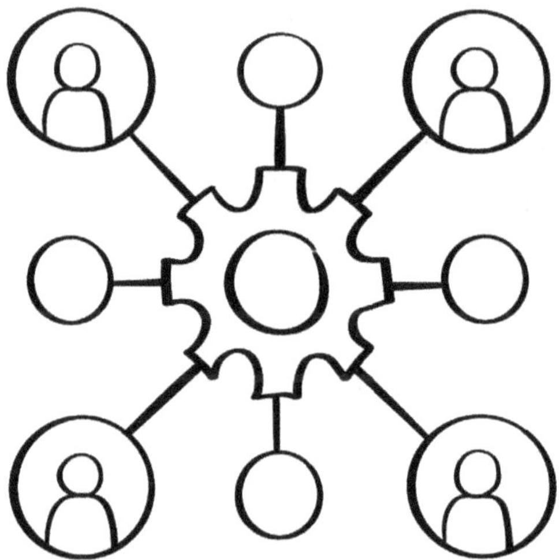

We finally need to understand the organisational context that is most likely to cultivate people who come to work to make a discretionary contribution.

This investigation needs to cover two areas of enquiry:

- *How the purpose of the organisation is articulated.*

The narrower and more mercenary the purpose of the organisation is seen to be, the less likely it is to solicit the discretionary contribution of its members.

- *How control is dealt with in the organisation.*

It stands to reason that a person who makes a discretionary contribution has the autonomy to do so. In the process of enabling this person, one must consider the degree to which systems, processes and structures either promote or frustrate people's initiative.

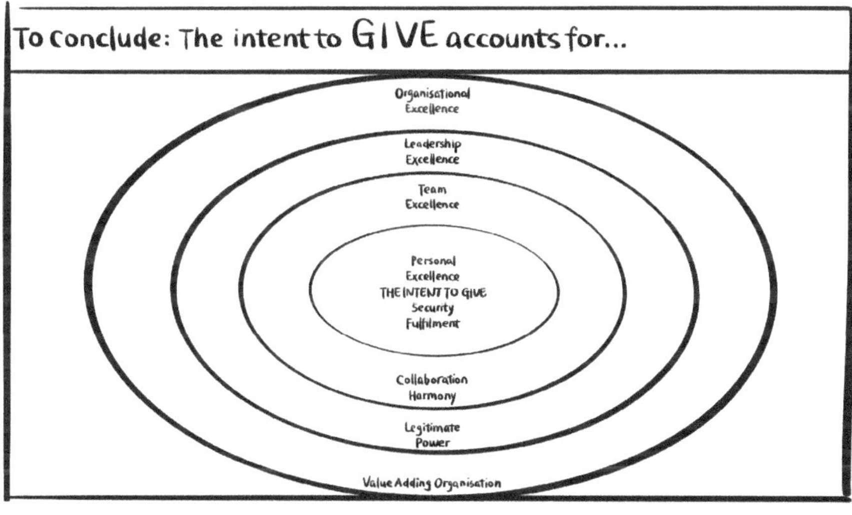

Chapter 2

Personal Excellence

In exploring the issue of the *culture of the organisation* and the *intent* of the individual, it is important to bear in mind that people can come to work with the intent to contribute irrespective of the toxicity or health of the workplace. In this sense, the intent of the individual to give has a more profound effect on culture than culture has on the individual's intent.

The reason for this is that the *intent to give* is what actually produces what people want from work. To make the point, I would like to examine what people aspire to, what concerns them and what they really seek to achieve at work. Over the years, we have asked many people why they go to work, and we have found that all the things they said can be contained in *four categories*:

Security

People would say things like the reason for them coming to work is to provide for their families, to pay the mortgage, to earn a living. If one explored their responses with them for a while, it becomes apparent that there is a real fear that is at the root of this issue. An insecurity that neither them nor their loved ones will be provided for if they do not earn a living by working.

Fulfilment

People refer to wanting job satisfaction. This is often associated with having a role where they can learn, be challenged and able to be creative. It is apparent that most people become uncomfortable with the idea of stagnation, of not developing as a person as they mature. Even if they do not necessarily wish to go up the hierarchy.

Power

While this is not necessarily a politically correct motive, it is true that status and significance can be very important to people. People could say things such as 'wanting to develop in their career' or 'get a senior job'. It has occurred to me that very few people are comfortable with the idea of dying "a nobody". We all want to be somebody. There is a competitive streak that runs through most of us.

Harmony

Many people also have very benign reasons for working. They feel, for example, that their work and the businesses that they serve contribute to the community or that they seek to make the world a better place by doing what they do. One may by cynical of the view, but very often this is the overriding motive that people articulate. I have been told by people that they have traded pay to have a sense of contribution at work.

Most people have the view that these four things, *security, fulfilment, power and harmony* are things they find at work. They need to go to work to fetch them there, so to speak. I would instead argue that these four things are not things that one can find at work, rather, they are things you take to work. They are things you manufacture inside your skin because every one of them is the product of your intent. It is possible to construct one's intent on two different variables: *'what one gets or what one gives'.* There are profound implications for all four of the categories of security, fulfillment, power and harmony with regard to which one of these two variables can make the basis of one's intent.

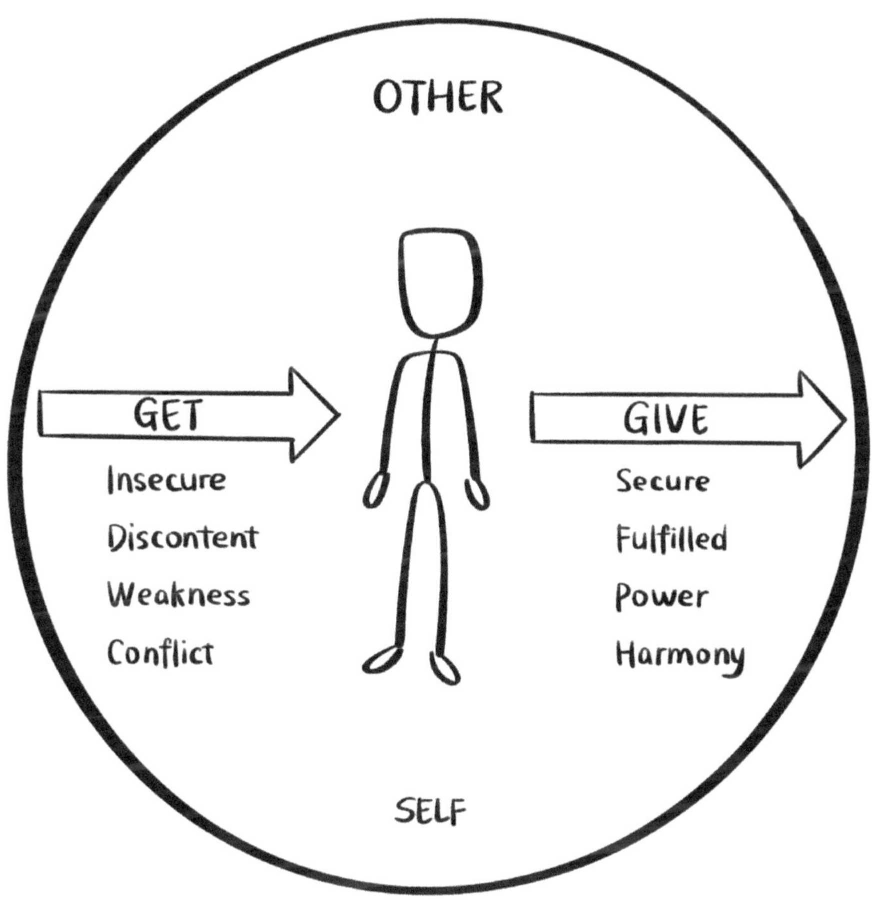

The Intent to Give and Security

What you get sits outside of your hands, the other has power over that. This suggests that if you base your security on what you get from the world, such as a salary or some assets, it is impossible for you to be secure because you are basing your security on something you have no power over.

If, on the other hand, you base your security on the quality of your contribution, because you always have power over that, you will always be secure. Some people know this. They are aware that the itch called insecurity scratches on the inside. They do not base their sense of security on something that a boss, or anyone else, has power over.

The Intent to Give and Fulfilment

From one point of view, exactly the same logic that is at issue for security is at issue for fulfillment. If I base my fulfilment on what I get, because the world rarely gives me what I want, I will be discontented. Whereas if I base my fulfillment on what I am giving, because I always have power over what I am giving, I will always be fulfilled. This understanding helps to make sense of two of the qualities mentioned above, namely that they seek to learn and to improve.

The Intent to Give and Learning

The intent to get is expressed in behaviour such as an inability to listen. When someone answers you back while you are trying to explain something to them, they are giving attention to their own agenda. For them to listen to you, they must suspend their agenda to give attention to the agenda of the other. That ability to suspend your agenda for the agenda for the other is called giving.

It means that you are able to ignore what is going on in the subject, or be subjective, and give attention to what is in the object. Be objective. This suggests that someone who cannot suspend their own agenda cannot learn, they cannot be open to new information. On the other hand, someone who can suspend their agenda is not presumptuous. They are open-minded, they can learn. Learning is a product of the intent to give. While it may be difficult, this has to be possible for a person who is in a toxic environment. Irrespective of how bad your situation is, it is always possible to remain curious about what you are learning.

The Intent to Give and Improving

The intent to give is also consistent with the idea of improvement. Consistent with the shift of intention from taking to giving is a shift of attention from outcome to process. An outcome is concerned with what one gets. A process is concerned with what one does or gives. One cannot improve anything by looking at a result, just like a cricketer cannot improve his game by looking at the scoreboard. Scoring better means playing better and playing better suggests that he gets his attention into the game, into his process.

The Intent to Give and Power

If I want something from somebody else, that person's ability to withhold what I want gives them control over me. They can manipulate me. They are strong and I am weak. To base my intent on what I want to get, therefore, makes me weak. It delivers me into the hands of the other. I have become a victim.

On the other hand, if I shift my intent to what I can give in the situation that I am in, rather than what I get, the other cannot withhold anything I want. This suggests they lose their control over me. I become powerful. My power is therefore the product of basing my intent on what I can give.

There is also a peculiar relationship between power and vulnerability. If one considered, for example, which of these two bosses has real power, the boss that you would work for because you had to and one you would work for because you wanted to, then most people would be of the view that it is the latter boss that would have the real power. If people are asked why? They would say it is because they are loyal to that boss, in other words, they give the boss power.

If you asked people to describe the boss that they would work for because they wanted to, all the attributes that they would describe would have themselves as the beneficiaries of the behaviour. In other words, the boss is there to give to them. Because people become loyal to a boss who is there for them, that leader has actual power, and they have that power because they are there to give.

The Intent to Give and Harmony

We have established that if I want something from someone else, that person's ability to withhold what I want makes them dangerous to me because I am in their power. They can manipulate me. Simultaneously, however, the fact that I am trying to get something from them makes me dangerous to them. They are dangerous to me and I am dangerous to them, and when we are dangerous to each other, we will be in a state of conflict.

If I change my intent from what I want from them to how I can be helpful to them, they can no longer withhold something I want, so I am safe from them. At the same time, precisely because I am trying to be helpful to them, I am no longer a threat to them. They are safe from me. When I am safe from them, and they are safe from me, we have harmony with each other.

We can see, again, that the last attribute which is ascribed to the person who is here to contribute, the desire to deliver to others, produces the harmony with others which many people desire to find at work. That harmony and the delivery to others it implies is a product of something that happens on the inside, one's intent.

To Conclude:

That which people generally want from work: *security, fulfillment, power, and harmony,* they will not find there. You manufacture those things in your own skin. These things are not things you get at work, they are things you take to work. People who experience those things experience them as an attribute of the intent to give. That intent to give translates into the primary building block of culture.

Every workplace, no matter how toxic, has some people who are like that, people who are comfortable enough in their own skins to be at work to contribute. If your fascination is about developing culture, then your fascination needs to be about enabling more people to be there to give. The important thing to understand in this matter is that these people choose to give. People who choose are people who are autonomous.

One can therefore not manage or control for an outcome that would deliver people who are like this. As everything that is truly human, this is fundamentally a problem of trust. Healthy cultures are the manifestation of organisations where people are *trusted* to contribute. They are not the products of a system.

This suggests that the fundamental variable that accounts for healthy *cultures* is not outside the individual. It is inside the individual. It is concerned with the shift of the individual's intent from taking to giving.

Chapter 3

Team Excellence

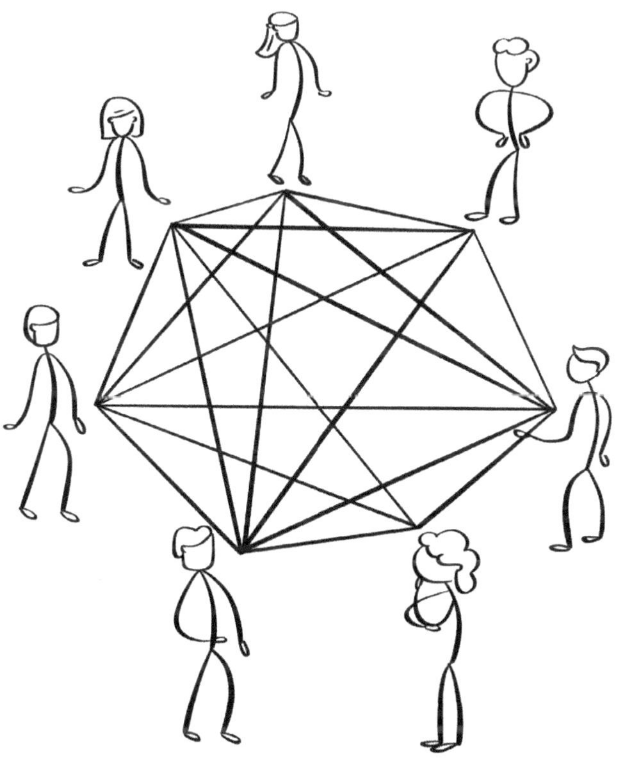

In an organisation with a robust and healthy culture, teams are characterised by collaborative behaviour. On the other hand, when an organisation's culture is toxic, the behaviour of members of teams toward each other will be fundamentally competitive. This will be expressed in issues like a dysfunctional emphasis on silos, meetings run in the spirit of win/lose by the participants and excessive cc'ing in email interactions. Once again, it is the intent of the individual that accounts for the culture of teams either being competitive or collaborative.

> Team members of collaborative teams deliberately set each other up to succeed.

In our previous discussion, we concluded that a person establishes harmony with those around them when they act based on what they can give. One of the expressions of this harmony is that the team that such an individual participates in becomes more harmonious. If one considered any successful sports team, like a soccer team, it becomes apparent that most of the work that happens on the field is not about somebody scoring; it is about somebody trying to set somebody else up to score.

This suggests that the 'spirit of being there to give' is expressed in how the team members deal with each other. The degree to which each member of the team is willing to set their colleague up to succeed and make them the star is the degree to which you have a team. When each member plays to be the star, one no longer has a team but a herd of cats.

Giving is about Generosity and Courage.

It is important to bear in mind that the intent to give is not about being nice; it is about being appropriate. If, for example, a hungry child asked you for food, then giving would mean to give the child food. If, on the other hand, you were a strapping young man and saw an old lady being mugged for her handbag, then giving would mean beating up the thug.

Generosity

While in both of these cases your intent was to give, the behaviour that you evidenced in the two interactions is actually contradictory. In the case of the hungry child, your behaviour was kind and gentle. In the case of the thug, your behaviour was violent and confrontational. This suggests that being here to give requires sometimes being kind, and we can refer to that kindness as *generosity*, and sometimes it requires one to be confrontational, and we can refer to that confrontation as *courage*.

Courage

This suggests that being here to give does not always mean being nice, it means being appropriate or acting consistently with either the generosity or the courage that is appropriate in the situation that you are in.

Taking is about Selfishness and Cowardice.

Selfishness

Where giving is about acting consistently with the generosity or courage that is appropriate in the situation you are in, taking is about getting one's logic wrong. If the hungry child asked you for food and you slapped the child, we would not accept your explanation that you were being courageous. If you grabbed the bag from the old lady and gave it to the thug, we would not be convinced if you said you were being generous. We would think you were cowardly.

Cowardice

This suggests that if the situation that you are in requires you to be generous and you act in a so-called courageous way you are not giving, you are being selfish. On the other hand, if the situation requires you to be courageous and you act in a so-called generous way, we would find you cowardly.

Generosity and Courage as a Member of a Team.

It is important to bear in mind that of the two elements of giving, generosity and courage, generosity is the primary element. If a person is here to give, it is likely that their primary engagement with others would be kind and generous and only where necessary, confrontational and courageous.

Being Generous with Colleagues.

A team member who is there to make their colleague the star would, in the first instance, affirm their colleague. They would establish the strengths of their colleague and they would, where appropriate, point those strengths out to others.

Further to this and as we indicated before, a key behaviour that demonstrates the intent to give is listening. To listen, one must be able to suspend one's own agenda for the agenda of the other. A team member who is there to make their colleague the star would not compete for airtime with that colleague and would intervene to allow the colleague to be heard, if necessary.

Being Courageous with Colleagues.

What is further true about a team member who is there to make their colleague the star is that they would have the courage to give the colleague feedback where it would be helpful to them, even in situations where the colleague would not want to hear what was being said.

While the conversation that ensues from this may be robust and heated, the courage that may be required is never an excuse to abrogate the primary requirement of giving, namely generosity. One gives the feedback with the intent to be helpful, not with the intent to hurt. Too often one finds people excuse blatant rude behaviour on the basis that they were 'just being honest'. Honesty is never an excuse for discourtesy.

Giving and Seeing Things As They Are

	GIVING	
	Inward Reflection	Outward Action
Secondary Element	Trust	Courage
Primary Element	Gratitude	Generosity
Root	Seeing Things as They Are	Giving Each Situation It's Due

Giving or acting consistently with the generosity and courage that are appropriate in the situation you are in can be described as giving each situation its due. It is about how one acts in the world, in the outward. This capacity to give each situation its due is based on another skill, which is seeing things as they are. It is not possible to act appropriately if you have not appraised the situation properly.

Just as the outward action of giving each situation its due has an inner equivalent, namely seeing things as they are, so too both generosity and courage have inner equivalents.

The Inner Equivalent of Generosity is Gratitude.

To be generous means to give away. If I give something to someone in the spirit of making an investment, my action can't be seen to be generous. When I am grateful, I recognise that I have received in excess of my due, which makes it easy for me to give to give away. Thus, my gratitude enables my generosity.

The truth of this is evident when one considers the effect on one's action when you are resentful, which is the opposite of being grateful. When I am resentful, I do not want to give anyone anything because I am convinced that I am owed, and that they should be giving to me.

Gratitude

Just like one's gratitude enables your generosity, so too your generosity enables your gratitude. If you only 'give' in the spirit of making and investment, you will assume that when somebody is giving you something, they are doing the same.

Resentment is the Opposite of Gratitude.

You will be incapable of seeing that they were giving to give away, which would not make you grateful. On the contrary, you are likely to be suspicious. You would think, 'What do they want from me?'

Resentment

This suggests that people who are generous with their team colleagues are also appreciative of them. The fact that they affirm that their colleagues give to them enables them to be generous with their colleagues. In fact, it is precisely because they are grateful to their colleagues that create the conditions where their colleagues will give to them. There is nothing more pleasurable than giving to somebody who is truly appreciative of what you are giving and there is nothing more distasteful than giving something to someone when their resentment makes them feel entitled to what you are giving.

The Inner Equivalent of Courage is Trust.

I can only learn that I can trust my colleague when I take a risk with that person and that person acts is such a way as to vindicate the trust I put in them. The risk I take therefore enables me to earn trust in that person. Conversely, once I have earned some trust in that person, it is easier for me to take a risk with them and to act courageously.

Trust

This suggests that my trust enables my courage, and my courage enables my trust. If I cannot trust the person to do what they should do, the only recourse I have is to control them. Controlling them means they will experience that I am trying to make sure that I get from them what I want. I am trying to take something from them. There is a difference between having something taken from you and giving something. People resist being manipulated.

Gratitude is the Key:

The elements of gratitude and generosity are orientated to the past. When I am grateful, I am grateful for what has happened. When I am generous, I give away what I have accumulated. On the other hand, trust and courage are orientated forward to the future. I trust things will not go wrong and I don't run away as the enemy comes over the hill. I behave courageously. This suggests that of the four elements of *gratitude, generosity, trust and courage*, gratitude is the key that enables the rest.

If, as a member of a team, I am grateful, in other words, recognise that I have been given in excess of my due, then it is easy for me to give to give away, to be generous. Further, should I look at the past and recognise that I received in excess of my due, in other words that I cannot account for my current good fortune on the basis of my own ingenuity, then it is easy for me to trust, to assume things will probably go well in the future. After all, if I recognise that things have gone well in the past, possibly despite of me, I can assume they will go well in the future. I can trust.

> The cycle of gratitude, generosity, trust, and courage is the basis on which any relationship is developed – not the least.

Teams are Built Incrementally:

If, in their interaction with other members of the team, a team member starts to act consistently with the elements of gratitude, generosity, trust and courage they introduce an adhesive which, over a period of time, starts to produce the stickiness and cohesiveness of the team. This stickiness presents itself as a spirit of collaboration that manifests in the team's effectiveness as well as in their pleasure in working and their pleasure in working together. The most powerful of these elements is gratitude and appreciativeness.

If, on the other hand, a team member presents a sense of resentment toward their colleagues, they will manifest selfishness, distrust and cowardice toward their colleagues, which will, in time, produce a failing team where the members compete with each other. The team will not hold together. It will fall apart.

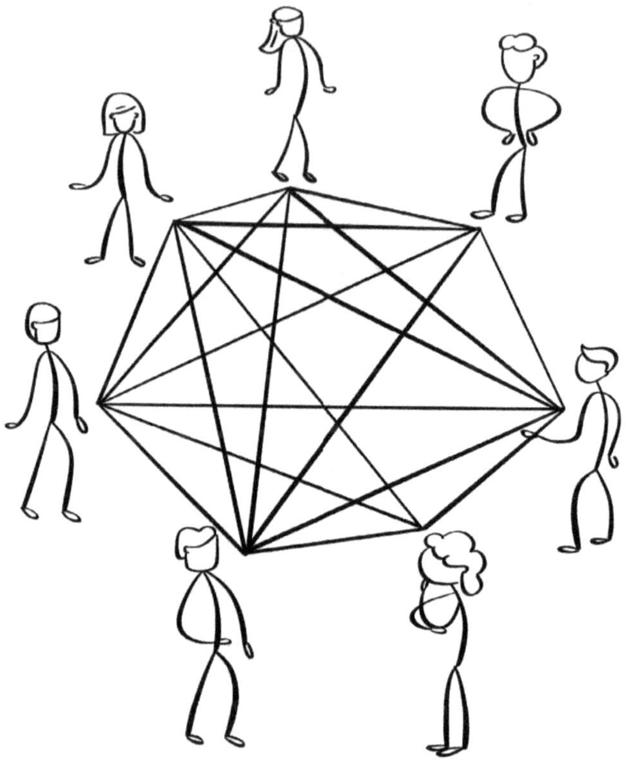

The intent of each individual on the team has this effect; It can either be an adhesive that binds the members, or it can be a solvent that dissolves the bonds between members. These adhesive or solvent effects are at play continuously, irrespective of the organisational context the team is operating in or how the team is led. These effects are also manifested and iterated or countermanded in every interaction between members of the team.

Further to this, a particularly authentic person, one who is truly unconditional with the contribution they make, will begin to build a bias to health in the team incrementally. This is because, as we have observed previously, that to act on what you can give makes you powerful and to act on what you want to get makes you weak. This holds true for any person on the team, even the most junior. These sorts of individuals, therefore, tend to become very influential on the team and can have a profound effect on the team over time.

This suggests that the giving of the individual accounts for both personal excellence and team excellence and is the heart of collaboration. This intent of the individual to give produces the collaboration which is the hallmark of healthy cultures, and can be accounted for independently in how the team is led or what the organisational context of the team is. It is possible to have a healthy team culture in a team operating in an otherwise dysfunctional organisation. Indeed, anyone who has worked in large organisations will recognise that this is true. Just as it is possible to have a dysfunctional team in an otherwise healthy organisation.

It is, however, possible to lead a group of people in such a way that will develop the intent of the individual to contribute, just as it is possible to create an organisational context which will encourage contribution.

Chapter 4

Leadership Excellence

While it is true that the *culture* of an organisation is the product of the intent of the individual, which ultimately sits with the individual, it is possible to facilitate the incremental move of people in the organisation from taking to giving by giving attention to both the organisation and how it is lead. Of these two, the most significant variable is leadership because, in my experience, people go by and large the extra mile for people rather than for organisations. In other words, if you want to account for the conditions under which people come to work to make a discretionary contribution, work because they want to, then you need to ask who the boss is and how they understand their role.

Over the last three decades, we have asked many leaders to describe how they understand their role by asking them to define what the word 'leadership' means to them. While there are some exceptions, most of the definitions offered can be reduced to the following statement: '*Leadership is about achieving a result through people*'.

Leadership is about achieving people through results.

How most people see leadership is, unfortunately, deeply fraught. If it is sincerely adhered to by the leader, it will produce a disengaged group of people who will only work because they have to rather than because they want to. We have the following thought experiment that helps to make sense of the difference between the boss people work for because they have to and the boss people work for because they want to.

Fred's boss tells him: *"Fred, two years ago I did what you have to do now, so go and do what I did".*

Joe's boss tells him: *"Joe, two years ago I did what you have to do now. It may be useful to you to take a look at what I did".*

If the question is who will work because they have to and who because they want to, then Fred will work because he has to, and Joe will work because he wants to. However, this is not just because the boss is being more dictatorial with Fred.

To really understand the difference between the two interactions, one needs to understand the difference in the intent of the boss. In Fred's case, the boss is trying to get a job done, and he is using Fred to that end. In Joe's case, the boss is trying to be helpful to Joe, and he is using the job that Joe is doing as his means to that end. Fred's boss is achieving a result through the person, Joe's boss is enabling the person through the result. Fred's boss is there to take, Joe's boss is there to give.

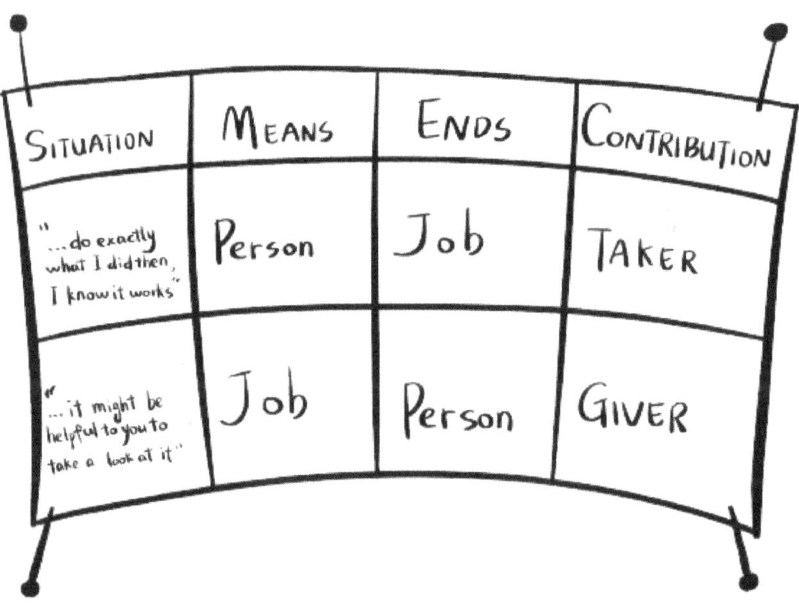

Coaches achieve people through results

The statement 'leadership is about achieving people through results' makes sense if one considers the role of a coach with regard to a team. If the coach of the soccer team, for example, told the players that it was his job to achieve a result and that he was going to use them as his resources to achieve that result, the players are likely to be very discontented. After all, it is not the coach who achieves the result, it is the players who do so.

The coach's job, rather, is to coach the player. The coach's product is an enabled player. This does not suggest that the coach has no interest in the game that is played or the result. Clearly, the coach goes to the game and is keenly aware both of what is happening on the field and what is on the scoreboard. However, what is happening on the field and what is on the scoreboard is not the coach's job. They are the means to do her job, which is to coach the player.

The coach's product is the player. The player's product is the result.

When the leader inverts means and ends in this way, they do not use people to achieve a result but they use the result as their means to enable people; they have shifted the intent of the reporting relationship with their subordinates from being there to take from them to being there to give to them. This is the most powerful shift that accounts for the shift of people for that leader from taking to giving. In my experience, when this penny has dropped into the consciousness of a leadership team, the organisation invariably takes off. The reason for this is that the people are now there to give. It stands to reason that people will not give to takers.

What People Want from a Boss

What exactly the leader should do becomes apparent when you explore the idea of the kind of boss people would work for because they want to rather than because they have to. Over the last four decades, we have asked many thousands of people from many walks of life and from very different parts of the globe this simple question: 'Describe the boss who you would work for because you wanted to'. All the content that one would elicit by asking this question can be placed in *two* broad categories: *Care* and *Growth.*

The Boss Who Cares for People

The category of care is the softer of the two categories. It would include elements such as being approachable, kind, empathetic, helpful, protective, respectful and listening, to name but a few. What is important about this category is that it does have an unconditional sense to it. What people are really saying is that the boss they work for because they want to is sincerely there for them, not just to get something out of them.

This sincerity is demonstrable by things such as the boss' ability to listen, in other words, to suspend their agenda for the agenda of the subordinate. Another example of this unconditional element would be something like the boss being supportive. It is very important for people to know that their boss will not throw them under the bus when it would be expedient for them to do so.

The Boss Who Grows People

Further to this kind theme mentioned above, people would also refer to tougher elements, such as the boss being honest, fair, and giving feedback. Clearly, if one worked for a boss who was always honest with you, that boss would not always be nice. Sometimes they would say things that would be quite upsetting to hear. The question would then be why you would want to get the honest feedback if it would upset you? You would want it because you know it is for your best, for you to learn and to grow.

This growth theme is also apparent in other things that initially don't sound quite so confrontational. For example, I often hear people say that they would want to work for a boss who would not interfere but would let them get on with the job, or empower them. What is apparent, though, is if that the boss did that, then the subordinate becomes accountable, which is tough. The boss is, however, treating them as an adult. The boss is growing them.

Care and Growth, and Legitimate Power:

What is truly remarkable about these care and growth criteria is the consistency whereby they are adhered to. Of all the thousands of people from all over the world who have answered the question, 'who is the boss you would work for because you wanted to?', we have yet to find a single element that you cannot ascribe to one of the two categories: CARE or GROWTH. We need to account for this consistency.

The first thing that becomes apparent if you work for someone because you want to is that you implicitly give that person the right to ask you to do things or to exercise power over you. This suggests that these care and growth criteria are the universal criteria for legitimate power. That this should be the case becomes apparent when you examine the following:

The first relation of power that one had with any other person in one's life is with one's parents, and in so far it is the first relationship.

It is a principle relationship. In a sense, one can deduce the principle of a matter by examining the first manifestation of the matter.

What is apparent in the relationship between the child and the parent is that the two are not equal, there is a very definite sense of hierarchy in the relationship. However, that hierarchy or inequality has a purpose, and the purpose is that the parent should *care* for and *grow* the child.

The job of the big one for the little one in any relationship of power is care and growth.

When the big one acts consistently with this criterion, the big one is doing with power what power is there for. Their power is legitimate.

The principle we glean from this is that:

Any relationship of power is legitimate if the aim of that relationship is the care and growth of the subordinate.

Legitimate Power and Control

If we assert that what makes the power of the leader legitimate is that they care for and grow the subordinate, it suggests we have a skeptical take on control. After all, grown or empowered people have autonomy, they can make decisions. One could even go as far as to say that power and control are opposites.

The boss with real power is the boss people work for because they want to. That boss is powerful because the people are loyal to them. It is in the Joe interaction where you say to Joe, 'two years ago I did this job, take a look, it may be useful' that Joe becomes loyal. Not only that, Joe is accountable. He has control over what is being done.

Empowered People are Accountable

When you say to Fred, 'two years ago I did this, do what I did' you, the boss, are accountable. You are controlling Fred. This suggests that you can only have real power based on the degree to which you are willing to forgo control.

Care and Growth is Concerned with an Incremental Suspension of Control

The less mature and able a person is, the more appropriate it is to control that person. One does not allow the same degree of autonomy to a child as you do to an adult. A child, for instance, may not legally drive a car, whereas an adult may. Growth is by its nature an incremental process. Therefore, to empower or grow a person requires an incremental suspension of control.

Empowerment and Means, Ability and Accountability

In each increment of suspension of control, there is a rule of thumb which is consistent with the dictum 'don't give a person a fish; empower them to fish'. If I was not at all able to fish and you wanted to empower me to do so, the first thing you would give me would be, the *means* to do so. This would probably include a hook, some line, bait, sinkers, a license and so on.

You would also need to make me *able* to fish. You would teach me how to bait a hook, where to cast, what the habits of the various species that I would want to catch would be, and so on. You would also teach me why I should fish by indicating that I will not only be fed for a day, but that I could feed my family over the long term.

However, assume you have comprehensively given me all the means and ability I required to fish, but I was also a very lazy person. You, on the other hand, had a freezer full of fish, and said to me 'Don't worry, if you don't catch a fish, I will give you one from my freezer'. Under these conditions, I would not be very engaged in this fishing escapade.

This suggests that there is a bloody-mindedness that you need to evidence at this point. You need to say to me 'If you don't catch a fish after this, *starve*'. You need to hold me accountable for what I have been entrusted with.

This suggests that empowering a person means to do *three* things:

- To give the person the means to do what is required of them.
- To make them able to do what's required of them.
- To hold the person Accountable.

In an organisational context, means would include giving someone the resources, the tools, the authority and the information to do the job. Further to this one would also give the subordinate your time if you were the boss. Consistent with the coaching analogy, a coach cannot coach a game she is not watching.

Care and Growth requires the presence of the leader.

Consistent with the idea of ability is, firstly, to ensure that the person knows *how* to do what is required of them. More importantly, they also need to know *why* they should do what is required of them. This *why* is related to what we refer to as the benevolent intent of the job. In other words, what value do we add and to whom by doing what we do?

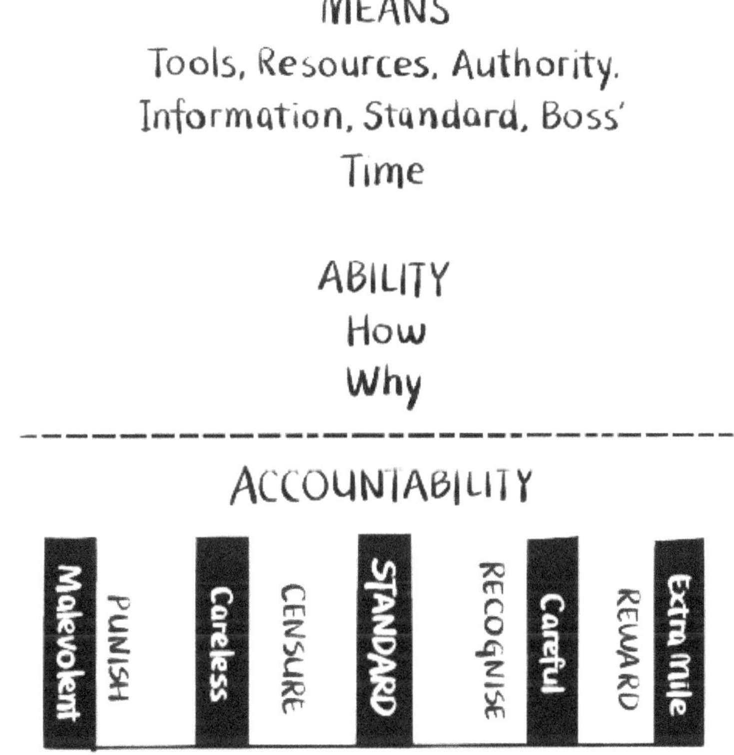

Finally, this issue of accountability is about consistent rewards and punishments. In the middle of the issue of accountability is the issue of standards. You cannot hold somebody accountable for anything if there is not a clear standard for what is required of them. A clear, known standard is part of the job, and someone's performance could either be above or below that standard. Someone's performance could be on or above the standard in one of two ways; they are either going the extra mile or they are careful to meet the standard.

Reward People for Going the Extra Mile:

When someone has gone the extra mile, it appropriate to reward them. This is not meant in the spirt of wanting to motivate the person, it is meant to fairly indicate the appropriate gratitude for what they have done.

Recognise People for Acting to standard:

When someone has done what is required of them, it is appropriate to say thank you. I often hear leaders say that when somebody is doing what is required of them, the leader need do nothing because the person is being paid for what they are doing. This is to suggest that the leader need not show basic courtesy because someone else is paying. It seems to me that the requirements '*please*' and '*thank you*' has not been abrogated just because you are at work.

Censure or Warn People for being Careless:

When someone has not acted to standard due to carelessness, it is appropriate that the matter is viewed as a disciplinary matter and that the sanction given be a warning. This warning could be anything from a verbal to a final written warning.

Punish or Dismiss People for being Deliberately Malevolent:

When someone deliberately acts contrary to the standard and has the means and the ability to act to standard, they should be dismissed.

How Leaders get Empowerment Wrong:

It is clear from the above that there is a logical order to the three elements of empowerment. You cannot hold a person accountable if you have not given them means and the ability to do what is required of them. In fact, to do so would be both harsh and unfair. We refer to this as the hard mistake. The *hard mistake* is to treat means and ability issues as if they are accountability issues.

There is, however, another mistake that leaders make. We call this mistake the *soft mistake*, which is to treat accountability issues as if they are means and ability issues.

Let's say, for example, you have somebody working for you who has all the means to do what is required of them and they are perfectly able to do what is required of them. Their performance, however, is below standard and in response you coach the person, or change the standard that is required of them, or give them more means. This is to treat an accountability issue as if it is a means or an ability issue. This is what we call the *soft mistake*.

Of the two mistakes, the soft mistake is the one that gets committed most frequently in large organisations. It is also the most destructive of the two mistakes because it is the equivalent of leaving the rotten apple in the barrel: If people are not held accountable, then over a period of time, more and more people start to perform below standard.

The soft mistake also gives rise to an incremental growth of control in organisations rather than an incremental suspension of control due to a phenomenon that one can refer to as the 'let's not witch hunt' syndrome. This 'let's not witch hunt' syndrome is manifested when something goes wrong and the boss decrees: 'let's not witch hunt, let's rather make sure it never happens again'. What that means practically is 'let's not establish who is accountable, lets rather impose another control'.

A small example would demonstrate the case: Let us assume that a group of executives at the same level of an organisation are all permitted to use a company issued credit card on company business. They have been training how to use the card, what to use it for and how to reconcile their card account with the company accounts. John Parsons, one of the team members, is found having used his credit card to pay for renovations to his home. Because his boss does not want to have a witch hunt, he sends John on a corporate governance course and he takes the credit cards away from everyone else. He does not hold John accountable; he deals with John as if John still has something to learn and he imposes a control which punishes everyone else.

In summary:

The most significant single variable that accounts for the degree to which the average person in an organisation is going to be there to make a contribution is how that person is led. A leader who solicits that discretionary contribution will be there to give to themselves, which, in the first instance, would mean they are not there to achieve a result through people, *they are there to achieve people through results*. The authority that they have over subordinates will be experienced as legitimate because they will be there to *care* for and *grow* them. This growth will be demonstrable in the fact that they provide *means*, *ability* and *accountability* to people, so that they are able to do their jobs.

Part of providing the means is to ensure that the organisational context that people are operating in is geared to enable the autonomy that is required for people to choose to give.

Chapter 5

Organisational Excellence

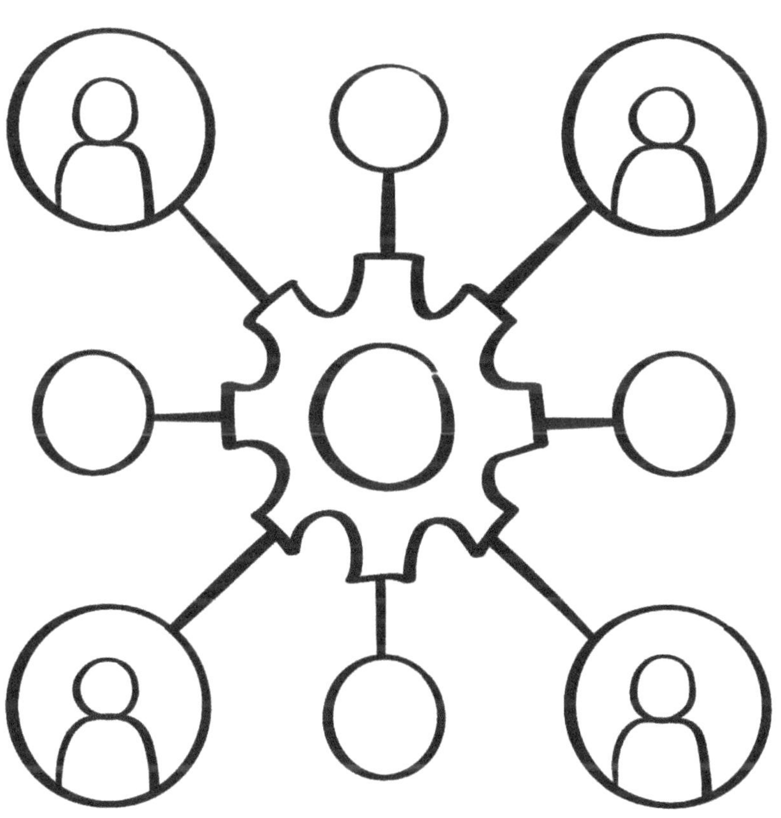

When looking at the issue of *'transforming culture'* there are *two areas of work* that need to be done when one considers the issue of *organisational excellence:*

Control, as expressed in organisational structure, systems and processes, needs to be set up in such a way as to enable the autonomy of the individual. If we argue that the success of the organisation is due to the individual making a discretionary contribution, then we must accept that it is only a person with an autonomous will who can make a discretionary contribution. If I contribute because of control exercised over me, my contribution is not discretionary, it is compelled. I have not given. Something has been taken from me.

The purpose of the organisation is framed as a benevolent intent. It answers the question 'why is what we do a noble thing to do'? or 'how does the world become a better place by us doing what we do'? This is by definition about understanding the purpose of the organisation as something bigger than the immediate interests of the owner or some other narrow and parochial concern.

The Three Assertions Regarding Control

I will preface the discussion that is going to follow by indicating that all three assertions regarding control are phrased somewhat provocatively. The aim of this is not to decry the value of control at all, it is to make one aware that control is not the virtue we often seem to think it is, and needs to be handled with circumspection.

Assertion 1:

The more control you impose the less control you have.

Every time one imposes a control on someone, you shift accountability for what is being done from the person who is doing the job to the person who is controlling the job. If, for example, there is a problem with the quality of my output and my boss instructs me not to put anything out unless she has checked it, she then takes accountability of the quality of what leaves the department and me. Assuming that she has done that with all of my colleagues in her team, she is going to be a very stressed and busy lady.

If we assume that the purpose of control is to have a predictable outcome then it appears to me that more often than not you will have a more predictable outcome if you let the person who is doing the job be accountable for the quality of the job. If, however, you seek to ensure that you have a predictable outcome by imposing a control; you disengage the will of the most important person, the person who is doing the job.

Assertion 2:

There is no such thing as a value-adding control.

There is a difference between enabling things to go right and preventing things from going wrong. The only thing control can ever do is prevent things from going wrong. It does not enable things to go right.

Another way of describing the difference is to contrast initiative and control. Initiative is what accounts for value adding behaviour. People have to engage their initiative to make a discretionary contribution. Control, on the other hand, disables or at least contains and limits initiative.

A useful metaphor for this is the relationship between the accelerator and the brake in a car. The accelerator is consistent with initiative. It causes the car to move. The brake, on the other hand, introduces friction and inertia in the system in order to slow the system down. Sometime this is important to do. A car without a break is a very dangerous thing. However, if one is attempting to enable initiative on a car that efficiently gets from A to B, then one clearly has to limit the number of controls one allows in the system.

Assertion 3:

Control is the organisational equivalent of weed.

Control is ambient in the matrix of an organisation just like the seeds of weeds are ambient in the soil of a garden. Nobody plants weeds. They grow quite spontaneously.

The intent to control is ambient in an organisation for two reasons:

- Most people in leadership positions have the view that it is their job to achieve a result through people. That suggests that there is a control bias to the very foundation of how they view their role.

- Many leaders have been brought up in a 'let's not witch hunt' culture, so when they encounter an exception, they more often than not impose a control rather than try to understand the accountability implications of what has happened.

These two conditions conspire to produce a situation where organisations spontaneously grow controls, like weeds, because most leaders at every level seek to impose more and more as time goes on. This growth of control eventually gets life threatening for an organisation. Just as a garden that is not weeded gets choked, so too an organisation that does not incrementally remove controls, eventually chokes under the weight of them. It becomes cumbersome and bureaucratic and, with time, is no longer nimble enough to respond to the demands of its market.

> **If you don't incrementally remove controls from your business you will incrementally go out of business.**

The business process re-engineering consulting industry exists because of this phenomenon. The problem is that very often the organisation has become so inefficient and bureaucratic by the time these consultancies get retained, that the surgery required is so radical that it traumatises the organisation to the point where it goes out of business. Alternatively, within a very short period, all the people who have been 'let go' are reinstated as consultants with higher salaries.

Control and Organisation

One could describe the purpose of the organisation to organise work, to render a sense of order and cadence to what gets done so that a coherent product or services gets delivered.

In order to organise the work one needs, first of all, to take the overall task that needs to be done and cut it into discrete, do-able bites of work. The visual representation of these bites of work you could call **structure**. The structure defines the discrete pieces work that get done.

Once the discrete pieces of work have been defined, one needs to connect them in a **system** or **process** that will serve as a conduit for the flow of value adding work.

While this way of thinking of organisation is helpful, the caution one needs to exercise is that it quickly becomes open to a machine metaphor in understanding the organisation which sees the person as subordinate and structure and system as superordinate. This undermines the autonomy of the individual, which we have argued is the key requirement for value adding behaviour.

Structure

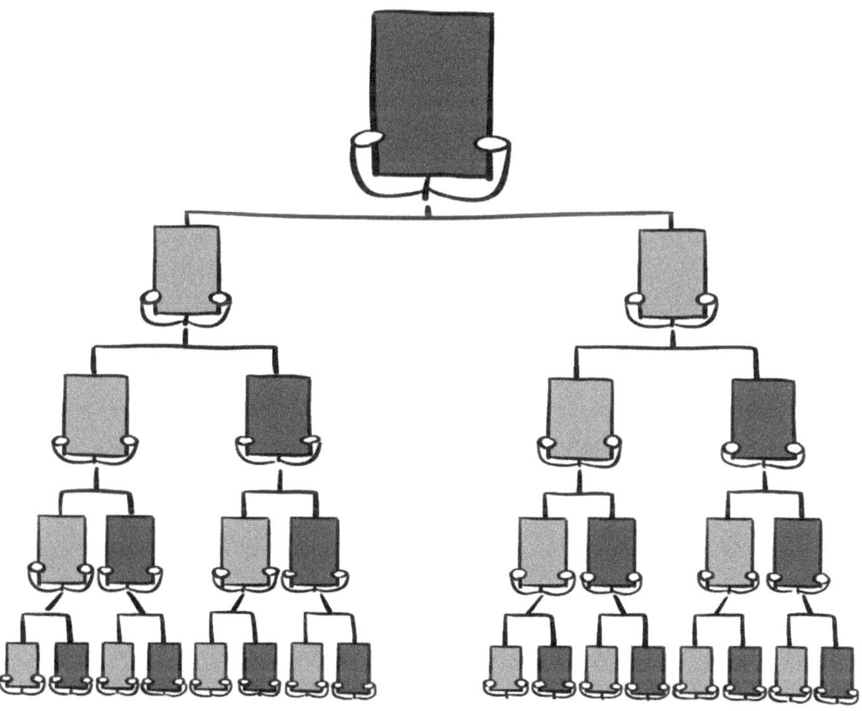

Considering that there is a connection between the degree of control that is exercised between people and the degree to which they will make a discretionary contribution, it stands to reason that more accurately one can define the discrete pieces of work that need to be done and the fewer handovers there need to be in order to complete a piece of work the more enabling the structure of the organisation will be. An enabling structure would minimise the number of times members of a team would need to refer outside their team or further up the hierarchy to execute their work.

The caution here is that this does not necessarily imply flat structures. Many executives I have worked with over the years seem to have had the view that flat structures are an end in themselves. This is not necessarily the case. Very often flatter structures come at the cost of minimising the ratio of leaders to subordinates in the structure, sometimes to a ridiculous degree, like 1/20 or 1/30.

Such a thin leadership structure overlooks the fact that the leadership of a work group, like the coaching of a team, is a legitimate job. It is a job that requires time and attention. As we indicated before, a coach can't coach a game they are not watching. Further to this, let us not forget that the contribution the leader makes is not just developing the competence of the team (*growth*). It is also caring (*care*).

Care takes time

Very often these flat structures are justified because key elements that are implicit in the leadership role, like care, coaching, discipline and reward, get stripped out of the line and delegated to a stand in on proxy function. This is what I refer to as surrogate management, which is to employ a proxy function to look after the people so line leadership can get on with their 'technical' job.

System

By *system,* I would understand the overall architecture of the functions that are orchestrated for work to get done.

In organisations that are big enough to have support functions, these functions very often become control functions in their own right, like the role played by a Finance function or an HR function or a quality function or a safety function. This is not to suggest that there is not a role for these functions, but they are important because they play an enabling role rather than a control role. Here are *two examples* to demonstrate this principle:

1. The Role of Finance:

In my experience, the finance function of an organisation is seen to be the custodian of the money which controls both budgeting and expenditure. This often creates the condition where line groups view their task to 'get things through the process' rather than to make financially sound decisions. If the finance function saw its role as developing the commercial acumen of line groups, they would enable sound decisions by these groups rather than making the decisions for them. It is important to leave the decision to spend and the accountability to spend with the line group.

2. The Role of HR:

Very often, employees in people's functions are given the role of 'looking after the people' and everything that entails, including things such as hiring, discipline, leave administration, remuneration and culture. All of these should be the accountability of line leaders, more specifically the immediate leader of any working team. It is more appropriate that HR people see their role as enabling line leaders to do these people related things, rather than doing them for them.

Processes

Empowering work processes are visual. They are deliberately designed to give an appropriate cadence or rhythm to ensure that team members meet at useful intervals and that the people in the room have the authority to deal with issues arising from the previous work cycle.

It is important not to view the assessment processes as measurement. The word measure seeks a number, which is not necessarily what one seeks to do when you are assessing a process. Let's say, for example, you are coaching me to run hurdles and you know that I need to lift my thighs parallel to the ground to clear them. As you watch me run, you notice that I am not lifting my legs high enough. By saying this your assessment of my performance is not subjective. It's perfectly objective, but it has not produced a number. When one assesses performance in an empowering way you asses it as *yes/no* against a standard.

An empowering organisation would also establish and hold leaders accountable for their leadership process. Do they care for their immediate subordinates? Do they give their subordinates the means, ability, and accountability to do what is required of them?

Benevolent Intent

The easiest way to explain what we mean by benevolent intent is by way of a thought experiment.

Which one of the following two statements of purpose delivered by a boss is likely to result in an operator at a pharmaceutical factory working because they have to or want to?

1	2
Work very hard because if you do you will help to make a shareholder very rich.	Work very hard because if you do, you will save millions of lives all over the world.
HAVE TO	WANT TO

It is clear that the first sentence would make the operator disgruntled and inclined to look for another job. There is no discretionary contribution here because the person feels used. The second statement, though, gives the person a sense that what they do is benign, it makes the world a better place. If we say that organisation succeeds because people make a discretionary contribution then we must understand that very few of us go the extra mile for a shareholder. If you want people to go the extra mile you need to give them a reason which is noble enough for them to suspend their self-interest.

This benevolent intent of the organisation provides an anchor for a line of sight for all other activities. Let's assume we are dealing with a janitor in this pharmaceutical factory. If the work that the janitor is doing is truly meaningful to the janitor, you should be able to tease the following logic out of him:

Boss: "Why are you sweeping the floor?"

Janitor: "So that we don't get dust in the product."

Boss: "Why should there not be dust in the product?"

Janitor: "Because then the product will be off spec."

Boss: "Why is that a problem?"

Janitor: "Well, if the product is off spec, the pills we produce will not work and we will not get to save the lives we are here to save."

Articulating a benevolent intent gives us the anchor for people to commit discretionary effort to pursuing the organisation's goals. It also provides meaning. The muscular and skeletal movements that are involved in the janitor sweeping the floor of the factory and the floor of the back porch of his house are exactly the same. Their significance, however, is completely different.

When the janitor sweeps the back porch of his house, he is busy with a purely personal affair that affects him alone. However, when he sweeps the floor in the factory, he is saving a life on the other side of the planet.

This understanding of benevolent intent enables us to see the real opportunity that working in an organisation provides us. It allows us to live lives that transcend our purely parochial concerns. Lives that are large, lives that have far bigger and more benign effect than when what we could achieve on our own.

About the Author

Etsko Schuitema is the founder of the Schuitema Group, a consultancy dedicated to the enhancement of human excellence based on the Care & Growth model.

Born into a mining family in South Africa, Etsko grew up in Johannesburg. After doing an Honours degree in Social Anthropology at the University of the Witwatersrand, he got a job as a graduate researcher with The Chamber of Mines of South Africa's Research Organisation.

Employed specifically by the Human Resources Laboratory of the organisation, his work initially focused on the issue of conflict on gold mines in South Africa. At the end of the overthrow of the apartheid regime, the mines were swept up in the upheaval that followed. The work he did led to the development of a framework for understanding trust in this very volatile environment.

Using this basis of this research, he was asked to head the Human Resources Laboratory's Industry Project and implement his insights. This is where the Care & Growth™ model originated. It was met with significant success within the mining sector. Such success in fact that Etsko left his role with the Chamber of Mines and, along with a group of colleagues, to establish a consultancy where this model could be more widely disseminated.

ALSO BY THE AUTHOR

ETSKO SCHUITEMA
intent
Exploring the Core of Being Human
SCHUITEMA
HUMAN EXCELLENCE GROUP

ETSKO SCHUITEMA
LEADERSHIP
The Care and Growth Model
SCHUITEMA
HUMAN EXCELLENCE GROUP

THE
MILLENNIUM
DISCOURSES
ETSKO SCHUITEMA

ETSKO SCHUITEMA
THE TWO SANDALS
Intention, Attention and the Journey
of Becoming Human
SCHUITEMA
HUMAN EXCELLENCE GROUP

ETSKO SCHUITEMA
THE POSTULATES
of the thematic
SCHUITEMA
HUMAN EXCELLENCE GROUP